Purpose's Missing Piece

7 Steps Process for Getting Your Top People Fill Your Talent Pool

DOV BARON

Copyright © 2018 Dov Baron

All rights reserved.

CONTENTS

Gratitudes	5
Meet Dov Baron	7
Introduction	8
The 7 Steps Process For Getting Your Top People To Fill Your Talent Pool	14
Why do you need to both elicit your organizations Driving Purpose© and implement an Internal Entrepreneur Program?	15
What is Driving Purpose©?	16
Purpose-Driven Companies	17
The Bottom Line	18
About Dov Baron	24

GRATITUDES

My sincere gratitude to everyone who has in their own way added to this book.

My gratitude to my wonderful, patient editor Woodeene Koenig-Bricker. Your ability to bring together my ramblings into something that even resembles good English while keeping it "Dov" is a genuine blessing to me, and the work I do.

My gratitude to my "Advisory board" for helping me pull in the multitude of ideas and help me see what is wanted and needed that I have the honor of providing.

Finally, thank you to you dear reader. Thank you for buying this book, spreading the word about the work we (my company and I) do. But most of all thank you for having the courage to work on yourself and your role in your company, your own inner circle, and in turn the world.

One red thread

No one does it alone! I'd like to thank my friends and board of advisers, each of you individually and collectively inspires me. Thank you for being a beacon of light shining my life and the lives that you impact.

We all have our blind spots, thank you for loving me enough to see mine, and share with me how I can better fulfill my own purpose in order to have the impact I came in here to have.

Renuka Baron - Certified Communication Expert. Licensed NLP Practitioner. Full-partner, co-facilitator, and mentor at Dov Baron International and Authentic Paragon Alliance.

Mark Levy - Positioning and Branding Consultant and Founder of Levy Innovation LLC. Writer for the New York Times. Writer/ Co-Creator of five books including the acclaimed "Accidental Genius: Using Writing to Generate Your Best Ideas, Insight, and Content."

Tony Grebmeier - Founder of multi-million dollar business INC 5000 business, Ship Offers. The host of BEFULFILLED podcast.
Joel Bower - CEO of Skirmish Strategies. Business Consultant to help drive momentum & leverage for growth.

Jim Bouchard - Corporate & Conference Speaker and Executive Mentor at Black Belt Mindset Productions LLC. Founder and Managing Editor at San Chi Publishing. Candidate for United States Congress

Joshua Miller - Master Certified Executive & Personal Coach. TEDx Speaker. Author of "I CALL BULLSHIT: Live Your Life, Not Someone Else's

Jared Nichols - Futurist, advisor, and faculty member at the University of Tennessee Haslam College of Business, in Graduate and Executive Education. The host of the podcast, "The Road Ahead: Small Business in the 21st Century,"

Damian Loth - Publisher at Men's Essentials Magazine. Partner at Media in Motion LLC. Official Sponsor of the Jamaican Bobsled Team.

MEET DOV BARON

A headline speaker for global conferences on leadership, influence, business and embracing change. Dov's interactive presentation style captivates and energizes audiences. His revolutionary thinking and communication style had him cited as one of Inc. Magazine's Top 100 Leadership Speakers to hire for your next conference, Dov Baron has been an independent leadership advisor to the United Nations (UN). A bestselling author and the top-ranking Fortune 500 podcast host.

He is also the leading authority on Authentic Leadership, and Leadership Succession or, as he prefers to call it, "Full Monty Leadership.and Leadership Archetypes".

Dov is the bestselling author of several books, including "Don't Read This…Unless You Want More Money!" and his latest, "Fiercely Loyal: How High Performing Companies Develop and Retain Top Talent." (In-Phase Publishing, 2015 ©)

He also writes for and has been featured in industry magazines including CNN, CBS Small Business Pulse, SHRM, Yahoo Finance, Boston Globe, Business in Vancouver, USA today, CEO, Entrepreneur and many more.

Dõv's international Leadership & Loyalty podcast is ranked the number one podcast for Fortune 500 Executives.

INTRODUCTION

Most enlightened organizations today understand the role and importance of purpose. When an organization knows its Driving Purpose© it provides clear direction for the organization, it understands its values and how to make decisions based on those values. What most organizations (even the ones that have done some work to find their purpose) are missing is not only does the organization need to articulate and live by it's own Driving Purpose©, but it also needs to assist the people within the organization discover, understand and live their own individual Driving Purpose©.

When the organization is operating via its own Driving Purpose© and the people within it are doing their jobs in alignment with their own that's when the organization will achieve new levels of engagement, sales growth, and market share.

This book is about uncovering and then facilitating purpose's missing piece, so that your top talent know that they are in the right place (within your organization) to find the purpose and meaning they crave.

PURPOSE'S MISSING PIECE

Richard, the founder of the company, beamed: "Not only are our people staying, our key players have become evangelical about who we are and what we do! I can't believe the change!"

Just a few months earlier, he was saying quite the opposite. He would hire great people, but inevitably they would bail before a year had passed. When I met him, he was defiant about the whole thing. "I do everything for these people and this is how they reward me—by leaving. I honestly believe I'm a great leader, but I just don't understand people these days. It used to be that people were grateful to have a job, but not anymore."

I knew what I was about to say would ruffle his already ruffled feathers, but if I and my team were going to be of genuine value it had to be said: "Richard, I'm sure that you are doing a lot of things right, but if you are losing great people and other great people are not lined up to work for you, it's you that's the problem." Without blinking he looked me right in the eyes, and I wasn't sure if he was going to scream and throw me out, or if what I'd said took him completely off guard. I continued. "Furthermore, if your corporate culture has supported leaders behaving like employees need you, or the company more than you need them, that's where the problem lays. If that's the case, I can see exactly what the problem is, and we can help!"

Richard sucked in an audible breath. He clearly didn't like what I said, (I didn't blame him... The Truth Often Hurts Before It Sets Us Free. I could make an educated guess as to what he was thinking. He most likely just wanted a quick answer that would make him "right" and "fix" the problem, but that's not how lasting solutions work.

We had been brought in to work with the organization because they were facing a potential crisis and Steven, the CEO, had been told to contact me by one of our previous clients who had struggled with keeping people loyal to her company. (We turned that around in four months.)

Steven asked me to come in and do a presentation on why great, or even good people don't seem to stick around. We began the meeting not by telling them what they should do, but rather by asking, "Steven tells me you have lost quite a few key people in the last year and that you seem to be having challenges keeping good people and replacing the ones who leave. Why do you think that is?

Richard jumped in without hesitation. "Because this younger generation are a bunch of entitled brats, they think they should be in charge and be paid more than someone with more experience"

"Thank you, Richard." I wrote the words entitled, need to be in charge on the whiteboard. "Anyone else have any ideas?"

Randy, the chief innovation officer, said: "Even though we are a real leader in the industry, I just think they get bored." I wrote bored on the whiteboard.

Elizabeth, the CFO, seemed agitated and snapped, "Well it's certainly not because of pay. We are consistently paying over the industry standard." I wrote salary and put a red line through it. I thanked her and continued around the boardroom.

A few more people spoke about what they thought it might be; much of which was restating in different words what the others had said.

Paul seemed pensive as I looked over at him and said, "You're HR. You are at the front line of dealing with this. What do you think it is?"

Paul paused and narrowed his eyes—a sure sign he was thinking--and then said, "I thought that it might be training and development, but we've increased that in the last two years and it's certainly slowed the issue down, but not enough"

I had written all the things they'd said on the board and then swiped them all away. I said, "All these things may be adding to the problem, but they are not the root of the problem." I took a long pause and asked: "What if talent, old or new, isn't the problem, and you—the leadership team—is?"

Richard's face began to redden and his jaw started to tighten. "You don't have to agree with me, but at least take a moment and allow me to share why I say that," I said. "It's the human condition: We all think any problem in our lives is the result of someone else. But the truth is nothing changes until we as leaders decide that the buck stops with us. That's why they call us leaders! The issue is not specifically generational, it's not specifically salary, and it's not even specifically training although each of those is a contributing factor."

I took a pause to allow the executive team to take it in. I explained that after we did our research, we found that the lack of loyalty in their organization boiled down to two key factors.

"Today's workforce wants to do meaningful work. Our research of your organization showed that no one from the front desk to the executive team could clearly state the Driving Purpose© of this organization. All of them knew what the company did. Some of them even knew the unique selling proposition. Many of them knew the mission statement and even some of the vision. But no one knew the "Driving Purpose©."

The second challenge when combined with the first pushes people out even when they want to stay. "The rigidity around systems in your organization is strangling innovation."

"So, if you are right, how do we fix this and quickly?" Richard's fists relaxed, I had his attention, because even if we don't like the truth there comes a point where we must face it or face the unfortunate consequences. In anticipation he started tapping his pen on a notepad.

I smiled and simply stated, "First things first. We need to elicit the Driving Purpose© of the organization."

Paul from HR perked up. "I've been reading Simon Sinek's It Starts with Why. Is that it?

Paul was on the right track. "Yes, Paul, that's a start. But what I'm referring to in saying the Driving Purpose© is what we call the "Why of the Why." It's the deep emotional reason each of you ended up right here right now. It's not fate, it's not magic. It's both deep psychology and physics."

I continued. "Here's why it matters. Today's workforce has at the top of their list for why they stay in a job is because the work is meaningful. Meaningful work is work where the individual feels an emotional pull to the Driving Purpose© of an organization because they either feel it's aligned with their own purpose. Or if they haven't found their purpose yet, by working for a company with a strong Driving Purpose© they have purpose by transference. The result is meaningful work that creates loyalty."

As I looked around the room I saw I was getting some validating nods, so I continued. "Second, the rigidity of the system needs to open up without collapsing in on itself."

Understandably, few puzzled frowns ensued. "Let me explain. We live in the time of the Internet. Much of your top young talent has grown up online. They know that they can have an idea, test it to see if it works and take it to market in very short order. Therefore, many of today's workforces are inherently entrepreneurial. They are always looking to upgrade their skills because they are wondering what they can do next."

"Yeah, we've worked that much out." The tone of Richard's voice indicated that I'd just given him justification for being upset with the disloyal workforce.

I smiled looked around the room allowing my eyes to land on Richard then I said, "What if they didn't have to take the skills, training, and development away from you?"

Richard was once again intrigued. "How do we do that?"

I leaned in. "Find a way to let them play out their ideas here."

Steven, who had been very quiet and attentive, suddenly jumped in. "What do you mean?"

"Create an entrepreneurial program inside the organization."

Steven looked curious and finally said, "Okay, show us what you can do for us."

We spoke for a little while longer and over following months we began working with the organization to elicit their "Driving Purpose©" at an intensive retreat.

From there we designed their "internal entrepreneur program." (Hang on. This is going to be important to you in a few minutes.) Four months into our work for this company, my partner and I were called into Richard's office to meet with him and Steven.

Richard started. "I have to tell you, that what you had to say at the beginning of that first meeting kind of rubbed me the wrong way. However, by the end and me telling myself to stop being so defensive, what you were recommending began to make sense. Although I did have my reservations as to whether it would work."

Steven jumped in. "You had said at the end of the "Driving Purpose©" process that we would likely lose some other team members. That was a pretty scary idea, particularly as I'd recommended you to come in and plug the talent leak."

"And now?" I asked.

"May I?" Steven said to Richard. Richard nodded and Steven continued. "For the first time since in the five and a half years I've been here, in a couple of positions we have a talent wait list."

I thought I knew what he meant, but I wanted to be sure. "What do you mean by wait list, Steven?"

"Not only are our people staying but also they have become evangelical about us. As a result, we have outstanding candidates on a waitlist to come on board." He continued, "It's a good problem to have!"

I think you would agree that a waitlist is a good problem to have. And that problem began with their Internal Entrepreneur Program. I said the "IEP" would become important to you. Well, that's because I'm going to gift the process to you right here in this special report so that you can immediately implement it into your organization.

The 7 Steps Process For Getting Your Top People To Fill Your Talent Pool

I'm about to reveal a process that many of my clients have paid tens of thousands of dollars to learn. It's my gift to you. Every client who has implemented this process has not only increased retention but also engagement. But here's the rub: You will have to implement! Here's how to create your Internal Entrepreneur Program (Intra-preneurial program) in your organization.

Gathering all your key people: Begin walking the whole team through each of these seven steps.

Step one: Start by asking this question: "If we gave you one million dollar seed money to start a business based on not just an idea you have, but something that would be of great meaning to you what would that business be?"

Step two: Listen carefully to all their answers. Have them write their ideas on a board where everyone can see them.

Step three: Ask each member of the team: "If we (the company) said 'yes.' how could what you just described be done by or within this company?"

Step four: "Knowing that our "Driving Purpose©" is (you see why that has to come first) X, how does your idea/product/service align with who we are at a purpose level?"

After you've listened carefully and taken in as much as you can (with zero dismissal), continue…

Step five: Looking only at other people's ideas, answer the same question: "Knowing that our "Driving Purpose©" is X, how does their idea/product/service align with who we are at a purpose level?" Again after you've listened carefully and taken in as much as you can (with zero dismissal).

Step six: Boil it down by asking "If you had to choose to work on a project that was not your own, which would you choose?"

Step seven: Set up work time each week for the internal entrepreneurial teams to come together and work on the highest rated project.

The result of implementing this 7 step process will be tremendous engagement of the your key people. They will be empowered to create within the framework of the organization (potentially creating products and services), and at every step of the way they are becoming more familiar with, more connected to, and more driven by the organizations Driving Purpose© being in alignment with their own.

Those are just some of the benefits…

Why do you need to both elicit your organizations Driving Purpose© and implement an Internal Entrepreneur Program?

A creeping crisis is infecting companies, organizations, and leadership today. Over the next twenty years, this crisis will slam the bottom line of companies large and small harder than any recession in recent memory.

To put it bluntly—companies are hemorrhaging talent at an unprecedented rate.

The average company spends 1.5 to 2 times the annual salary of an employee in training and development. That wouldn't be a problem except the average Millennial employee is looking at a tenure of 1.2 to 2.4 years at the outside. That means expensively trained employees walk away before the investment the company made in them even begins to pay off. What's even worse is that the employee trained at one company now will leverage all that training for a better position...often with a competitor.

This crisis can be stopped. But not just by slapping a Band-Aid on the bleeding. Business owners, regardless of the number of employees, can find and adapt strategies to create adherence with their employees, virtual contractors, and all stakeholders. It isn't easy, but it can be done. What it requires is rethinking traditional concepts around leadership and loyalty.

I consult with leaders around the world on how to keep their talent, especially top millennial talent. I engage with leaders from the banking and financial sectors to leaders of multi-generational business families. I work with companies that range in size from a few million to hundreds of millions. I assist companies that are focused on high tech innovation all the way through to construction. I present 25-30 times a year, to English-speaking audiences in the USA, Canada, Australia, and Europe. My audiences are usually leaders of companies at the $3-$100 million value, who are seeking to increase loyalty and engagement.

What I've seen, regardless of size or industry, is that most leaders do not understand that what drives today's workforce is something completely new. As stated earlier; the days of simply paying top talent more in order to keep them loyal no longer works. Money remains a motivating factor, but only to a point.

What is Driving Purpose©?

We all have days where it's hard to get out of bed. For many people, the demands of work and life in general can seem overwhelming on a daily basis. According to The Engaged Workplace, Gallup conducted studies over three years (2017) and learned that fewer than thirty percent of people in the workforce are fully engaged. Forget about springing out of bed; it's hard to even crawl out of the covers to go do something that has little meaning beyond providing the means to pay the rent. Yet miraculously, some folks, no matter what is going on, find a way to not only get out of bed but indeed do spring out of bed. What do they know (or have) that so many others don't? The answer is purpose.

Purpose is the key ingredient of a genuinely authentic leader who inspires loyalty. Purpose is also the highest value asset of a sustainable organizational culture. Purpose, when realized, is woven into the fabric of an extraordinary leader and it becomes the unseen, yet ever-present engine that drives an organization. For a new, emerging company and/or companies who recognize the need for a fresh start, Purpose can be a strategic starting point and an organic attractor of both top talent and customers. In what can appear to be a hyper-competitive environment, there is no greater differentiator than Purpose. For an individual and or a company to thrive in today's global marketplace, we need to infuse Purpose in all that we do.

Purpose-Driven Companies

Today we are seeing the rise of more purpose-driven companies. All the way back in 1994, Jim Collins, a former teacher at Stanford University's business school, and Jerry I. Porras wrote the New York Times Bestselling book Built to Last: Successful Habits of Visionary Companies. They took an in-depth look into eighteen truly exceptional and long-lasting companies and studied each in direct comparison to one of its top competitors. Throughout the book, the authors asked, "What makes the truly exceptional companies different from the comparison companies and what were the common practices these enduringly great companies followed throughout their history?"

They were all purpose-driven organizations.

In a survey titled "The Business Case for Purpose," a team from Harvard Business Review Analytics and professional services firm EY's Beacon institute (2016) declares: "a new leading edge: those companies able to harness the power of purpose to drive performance and profitability enjoy a distinct competitive advantage." Ninety percent of respondents in the study said their company understood the importance of purpose, but less than half thought it ran in a purpose-driven way. In every organization, whether its people realize it or not, "there is a systemic relationship between purpose (what we are here to do), measures (how we know how we are doing) and method (how we do it)." Eighty-four percent of executives believe an organization that has shared purpose will be more successful in transformation efforts.

Finding the true Purpose of an organization is about finding the primary drivers of the founders, leaders, and executives of that organization. In doing so, they become emotionally bound to it. Essentially, purpose is not found, it is elicited from the deep emotional drivers of the people involved.

The pursuit of Purpose, alongside the pursuit of profit, mobilizes people in a way that pursuing profits alone never will. An organization or a person without Purpose manages people and resources while an organization with Purpose inspires, engages, and catalyzes its people and resources. Because true purpose is elicited by discovering the primary drivers of the key players it becomes the psychological glue of the organization.

That is why this book focuses on purpose, what it is and how to create it.

The Bottom Line

Business at its bottom line is about just that—the bottom line. If companies don't make money, they are gone. However, more and more organizations and the leaders within them want to have an inspiring purpose for why they do business. This is partly because leaders are not stupid; they can see the writing on the wall and even though we may be in awe of the massive profits of companies like Monsanto™, not many people are willing to reach that financial success by having to live with the title of "the evil corporation incarnate."

Moreover, leaders who have scaled the rocky terrain to climb Success Mountain and are really honest about it know that being part of an inspiring, purpose-driven organization makes coming to work better. It feeds the soul. As a bonus, it's a great way to attract, engage, and keep top talent. In other words, purpose-driven companies are a vital element of generating fiercely loyal talent pools.

The world of business has changed vastly resulting in social and market demand for CSR (corporate social responsibility). However, CSR cannot be in place to pacify customers, employees, strategic partners or even the media as a way to gain good PR. Here's why: when corporate social responsibility is absent, it doesn't take long before customers and top talent start to vote with their feet and go somewhere else.

Many organizations today are experiencing that even when they find top talent they often don't stay. As stated earlier: The average Millennial employee is looking at a tenure of 1.2 to 2.4 years at the outside. The challenge is so often double edged in that it's one thing to lose top talent it's a whole other level of challenge when you can't find people at that level (or greater) to replace them. Again money is very often just not enough of a motivating factor for the Millennial workforce. Meaning/purpose however, is that driving force!

The purpose driven organization operates from a very different perspective than the purely profit driven organization. An organization that has not found its purpose or is not strategically aligned with purpose will likely drift on the tides of what the marketplace is telling it to do, and as a result can become very quickly unfocused and adrift in a sea of competition. The purpose driven organization by its very nature is outside of competition, because no one is doing what they are doing from the place they are doing it.

Meaning in an organization is expressed in two ways: It's in that the organization understands its overarching purpose above and beyond profit. Then the missing piece is that the organization gives its people the space to not only do their jobs, but also to intra-preneurially express themselves and their own driving purpose within the organization.

More and more organizations have come to the realization that a lot of their ills can be cured through operating with purpose. In fact there are many great books out there that start into the process like Simon Sinek's "Start With Why" and Lisa McDonald's "Selling with Nobel Purpose" and many other amazing titles. But what a lot of organizations are missing is that they are only looking at purpose from a single standpoint, it's like they are unknowingly leaving part of the equation incomplete. An organization needs to understand, express, eat, sleep and breath its purpose and in so doing make it decisions particularly in the context of hiring based on its Driving Purpose©.

The piece that is so often missed is that the organization needs to recognize that the individuals within the company also need to express their own purpose. Finding a way for employees to do that inside the organization create a massive competitive edge for that organization. This allows your people to not only grow but also to allow your talent to find the real meaning they are looking for in their work life.

If your organization is missing either side of the equation: The Organizational Driving Purpose© or creating space for talent to find and express theirs, the costs will be high. Not only will profits be hindered, but also the expanding lose of loyalty, which will be exponential can become crippling. If the company itself lacks purpose it will drift and react, for that matter so will employees.

Furthermore, when the people within the organization are not given the room to find and express their own purpose they start to feel like drones and the work they do begins to feel meaningless. When this happens your people will become dispirited because they will feel an important part of who they are is being repressed. Despite what we might want to believe money (paying them more of it) is not enough. This is because your employees are trading more than their time or skills; they will feel like they are trading their heart and soul for a paycheck. The result is initially disengagement, then if you are lucky they will leave at the first opportunity, if you are not so lucky they will stay and become actively disengaged, essentially working against the company by eroding the morale of those around them.

To clarify: There are two sides to the purpose coin; one is the organization's purpose and the other and so often missed; the individual employees purpose. For an organization to flourish both must be elicited and fulfilled. If either side is missing there will be problems with engagement, morale growth, and in turn profit.

Beyond keeping top talent loyal, other reasons to operate a purpose-driven organization include:

• Increased growth: S&P 500 Research shows that between 1998-2013 the average company on the S&P 500 experienced 118% growth. While according to Jim Collins, and his co-author Jerry I Porras in Built to Last, purpose-driven organizations experienced 1681% Growth.

• Shared values: 64% of consumers point to shared values as their main reason for working with a brand.

• Responsible operation: 90% expect companies to operate responsibly to address social and environmental issues.

• Social responsibility: 84% of consumers say they purchase socially responsible products whenever possible.

• Better performance: Companies with engaged employees outperform the competition by up to 202%.

Meaning (or the desire to be connected to, associated with a purpose) is the number one driving force in today's millennial workforce.

PURPOSE'S MISSING PIECE

So now let me hand you the mic:

- Have you found the Driving Purpose© of your organization?

- What are you doing (that works) to assist your people in finding their own Driving Purpose©?

- What are you doing (that works) to have your people become evangelical about your organization?

- Are you challenged with keeping your top talent?

- Have you as a leader found your own Driving Purpose©?

- Have you found your Corporate Driving Purpose©? (This is NOT a mission or vision statement)

- Do you have an Intra-preneurial Program in your organization?

- What might happen if you did what it takes to elicit your Driving Purpose©?

And finally:

- Are you committed to discovering your own and or your companies Driving Purpose©?

- What about building an Internal Entrepreneurial Program?

Our simple question is:

How can my team and I help you?

http://FullMontyLeadership.com/consulting

http://FullMontyLeadership.com/speaking

I work privately with leaders who are committed to serving at the highest level by being the very best version of themselves. I work with organization who are committed to serving not only their customers, partners, teams, and customers but also their communities and wherever possible the planet.

I also present 35-40 times a year, to English-speaking audiences in the USA, Canada, Australia and Europe. My audiences are usually leaders of companies at the $3-$100+ million value, who are seeking to increase loyalty and engagement.

ABOUT DOV BARON

Dov Baron: Twice cited as one of Inc. Magazine's Top 100 Leadership Speakers to hire, also cited in the Meeting and Event Professionals Guide to The Top 100 Motivational Speakers and Named as one of the Top 30 Global Leadership Guru's.

Dov is a man with a finger on the pulse of the evolving world of NextGen leadership.

He is a bestselling author of several books. His latest book is Fiercely Loyal; How High Performing Companies Develop and Retain Top Talent. He is the host of the national (US) TV show "Pursuing Deep Greatness with Dov Baron" on ROKU TV, and the host of the Number One Podcast for Fortune 500 Listeners (globally) "Dov Baron's Leadership and Loyalty Show" on iTunes and is carried on FM & AM Radio Stations across the US.

He also writes for and has been featured in many industry magazines including being featured on CNN, CBS Small Business Pulse, SHRM, Yahoo Finance, Boston Globe, Business in Vancouver, USA today, CEO, Entrepreneur and many more.

Dov Baron has been speaking internationally for over 30 years. Dov Baron has had the honor of presenting for many esteemed audiences including; US Air Force, The Servant Leadership Institute, The World Business Conference in Tehran The State Department, and The United Nations. He is considered by many as a leading authority on Authentic Leadership. Dov is also the founder of Full Monty Leadership and The Authentic Speaker Academy for Leadership.

Outside of his speaking and training, Dov works privately with multi-disciplinary leaders and executive teams to build the bonds that create organizational cultures that become Fiercely Loyal.

Life-Changing Story:

In June 1990, while free rock climbing, Dov Baron fell approximately 120 feet and landed on his face. The impact shattered most of the bone structure of his face, disintegrating some of his upper jaw and fracturing his lower jaw in four places. After nine reconstructive surgeries, no external evidence remains of the damage; however, this experience was life-changing.

Before the fall, Dov had spent years building a reputation as a dynamic speaker and teacher in the field of personal and professional development, but it wasn't until years after the fall that he began to see the beauty and elegance of what had really happened – the return to his own CORE –what he calls his 'Authentic Self'.

Today

Today, Dov has been sharing his wisdom and expertise privately and on international stages with professional leaders for more than 30 years. Dov's influence has created a massive social media platform with over 200,000 followers via Facebook, Twitter, LinkedIn, Podomatic, iTunes, etc.

He has interviewed and worked with leaders featured on Oprah, Ellen, CNN, Fox, MSNBC, CBS, Huffington Post, Larry King, New York Times, Washington Post, Forbes, the Wall Street Journal and many other top-rated media.

Dov's "KIllTheKeynote" campaign to change the speaking industry went viral to over 5 million people on social media. He is now speaking for some of Europe's Dov Baron FullMontyLeadership.com 22 wealthiest families at Scone Palace, Next-Gen leaders with UnleashWD and the Legacy Show, and top American c-suite leaders for The #CSuite Network.

In addition to being an author and a radio host, Dov is also the leading expert on Developing Authentic Leadership and he is the world's only Corporate Cultural Momentum Strategist, serving top performance individuals, corporations and organizations to generate both exponential growth and fierce loyalty.

His passion mixed with humor and 'get to the point' no BS style are contagious.

Within moments, you will feel a genuine connection with a man who authentically walks his talk. Dov believes that the world needs more leaders who are Authentically committed to living their Purpose, standing in their truth, sharing their inner genius, and empowering others to do the same.

Dov's commitment is to take you by the hand and show you why tapping into your Authentic Self is the MOST important key to finding, developing, and retaining your top talent.

To engage Dov Baron for media interviews, one-on-one as an Impact Strategist, speaking at your events, or consulting at your organization, please write to…

Admin@DovBaron.com

or call +1-778-379-7517.

FullMontyLeadership.com

www.ingramcontent.com/pod-product-compliance
Lightning Source LLC
Chambersburg PA
CBHW070946220526
45469CB00007B/2532